THE COLORS OF MUD

Buffy Jo Grenier

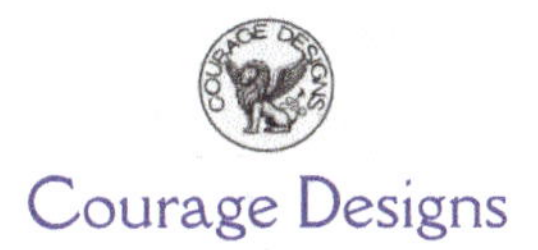

Courage Designs

The Colors of Mud
1st Edition

Written, art, and photography by
Buffy Jo Grenier
Contact: info@couragedesigns.com

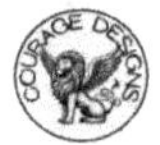

ISBN 979-8-218-46350-2

Printed in the USA by INGRAM SPARK

I dedicate this book to everyone who has
believed in me when I didn't, and the ones who
continue to do so.
To everyone who generously listened as I
vulnerably read that current moments
heartfelt
thoughts to them.
To my dad, who in his profound imperfection
still managed to encourage self love.
My mom from whom I learned how to be
strong, to hold on to my hat, and to keep
finding beauty in the world.
To my children who love and trust me in the
face of my own profound imperfections.
And to everyone who has feelings they don't
know how to quite put into words.
(I hope this is where you find them.)

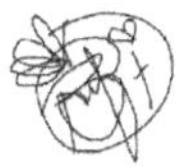

TABLE OF CONTENTS:

Chapters:

(Because who doesn't just *love* a chance to talk about themselves?)

PREFACE

This is where there is supposed to be some really self-important sounding words and statements about the book. And sometimes there's just random incongruent nonsense.

I just want to say hi.

Oh, well, and about the book? It's just my first in a series of collections of logophilic thoughts and emotions that have followed me through life. I invite you to remember your thoughts and emotions at the same times, while you're reading them..

Like....Jr. High...what a crap show that can be! And High school; Brick and Mortar schizophrenia dancing with mountain-peak clarity. Navigating that jungle-like climb into adult-hood with all it's blood and beauty. Life in general, pick a poison. Find an antidote.

We're all connected through these moments, even if we're not connected at all.

So, with these pages I offer you a high five, and a gentle pat on the back. Keep riding that bull, holding on tight to those horns! Or... just get off. Sometimes you've really no business riding a two thousand pound smelly animal anyway.

Read on.

Buffy

"There is a voice inside of you That whispers all day long,
"I feel this is right for me, I know that this is wrong."
...

just listen to The voice that speaks inside."

—Shel Silverstein

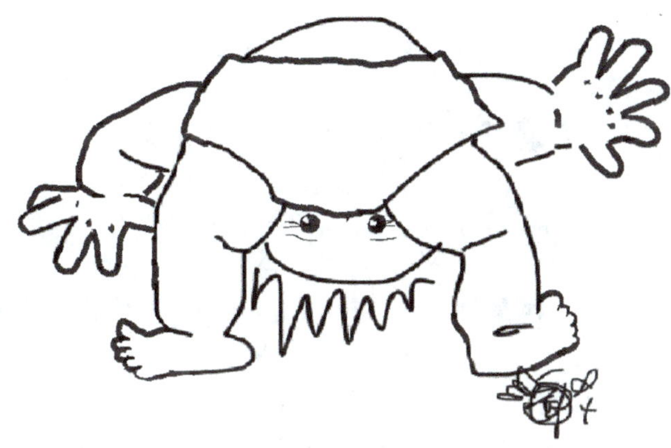

TO BE YOUNG AGAIN!
(I wouldn't repeat it for eleventy-billion dollars...)

<u>Take my will</u>

TAKE MY WILL, WILL YOU?
Please,
I don't want this thing
-Anymore –
MY CHOICE TO LIVE OR DIE
WHY?
Its all the same to me
Its easier to do what someone
Tells me to
It's much too confusing being free.
Free will
Who needs it?
It requires logic and care
No one heeds it.
GO AHEAD
Put a chain around my neck
and call me victim
BUT PLEASE!
please!!
Whatever you do –
Don't ask me to decide!!!

6-11-87
(19 yrs old)

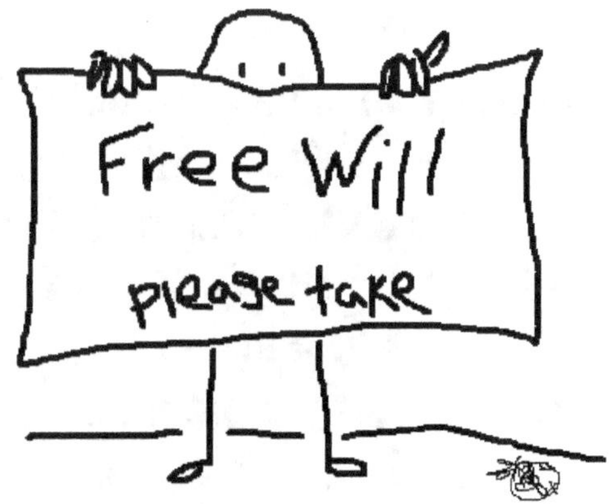

Free Will
please take

WHERE'S MY CROWBAR?

I am hiding behind a wall.
My wall.
I hide from what is on the other side.
Love.
Hate and violence.
They come from things, person, unknown.
Safe wall?
My wall was a protection,
It's turning into a prison.
The little miracles keep me from hysteria,
And my faith from giving up.
I will take apart the prison brick by brick...
...where's my crowbar?

1979
1st year of jr high
12 years old

THE FLESHY SUBSTANCE IN MY SKULL.

Scars are to see with, not the eyes.
For we see what we want to see.
The heart pumps blood through my flesh.
My heart does not symbolize my love for you.
My heart as a symbol is merely to say that my
heart beats for you; that I live only for you.
This is not so.
My heart will keep circulating blood corpuscles
through my veins and arteries if you were to
disappear.
What is it, then that can be this feeling?
Eyes are superficial. Limbs are for physical
purpose. The mind is the creator and the
defeater. The symbol of my love is the fleshy
substance in my skull.
How very romantic.

JAN. 1983
(10TH GRADE)

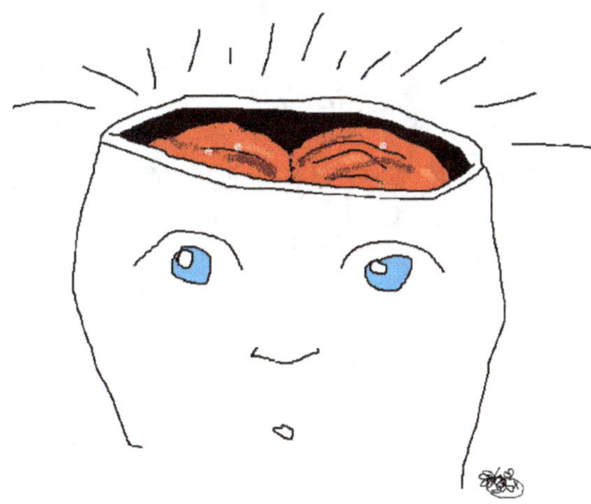

Dangerous dreams...

So it begins....
Another saga
Of the listless soul, the unforgotten
dreams.
Yes, unforgotten, in their cells.
And the guard, he knows...
He swings the keys before himself, looking
at the doors.
He is the listless soul, who has succumbed
to the safety of keeping these WILD
DREAMS at bay –
A solid, good paying job.
But, what if...? He shakes his head briskly.
Who's to say where his safety would go if
he were to set these wild dreams
free??

1987
(19 yrs old)

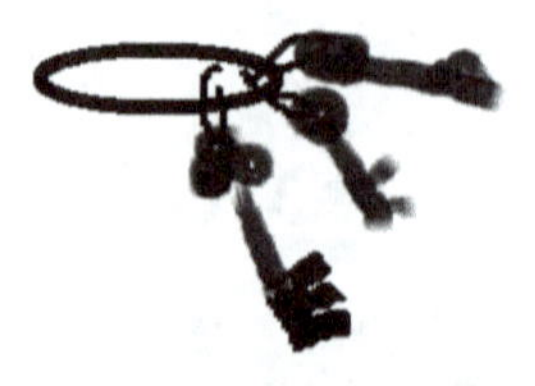

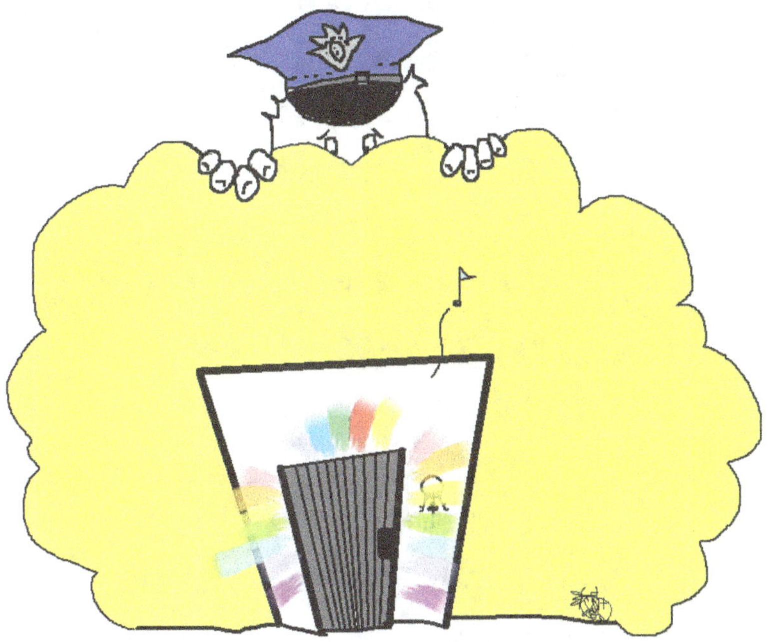

One 'Blah' for loneliness...

This Void
Or 'the emptiness'
As its been called
Seems to surround me
Wall to wall

I wish so much that it won't remain
For this loss of will
Drives me insane

It smothers my mind
With thoughts of sorrows
Making me regret the past
Making me forget my tomorrows...

1981-85
(sometime in highschool)

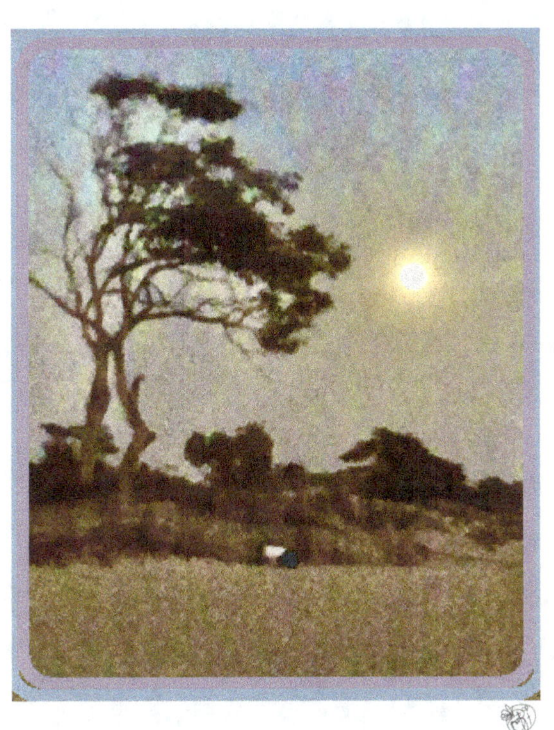

MAN OF WAR.

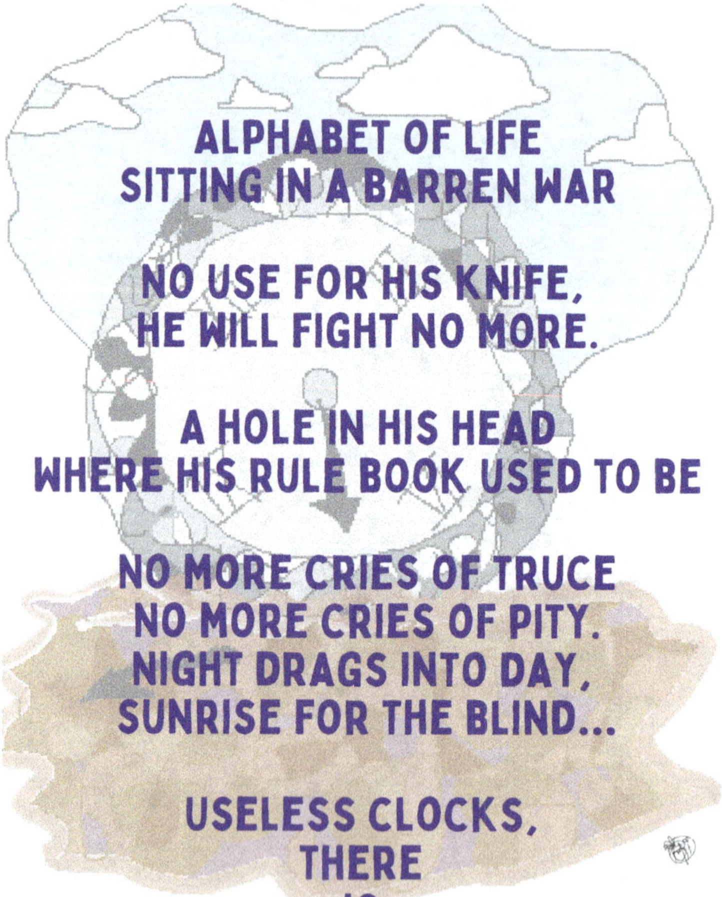

ALPHABET OF LIFE
SITTING IN A BARREN WAR

NO USE FOR HIS KNIFE,
HE WILL FIGHT NO MORE.

A HOLE IN HIS HEAD
WHERE HIS RULE BOOK USED TO BE

NO MORE CRIES OF TRUCE
NO MORE CRIES OF PITY.
NIGHT DRAGS INTO DAY,
SUNRISE FOR THE BLIND...

USELESS CLOCKS,
THERE
IS
NO
TIME...

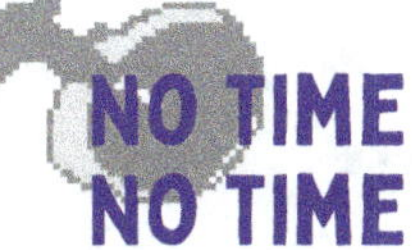

NO TIME
NO TIME

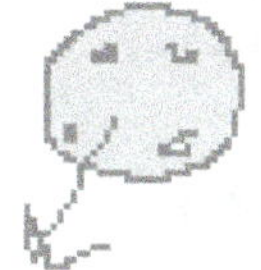

NO TIME TO LIVE

NO TIME
NO TIME

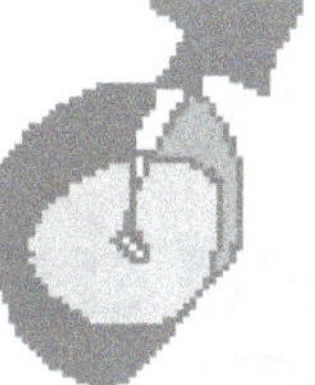

TO RECONSIDER

NO TIME
NO TIME

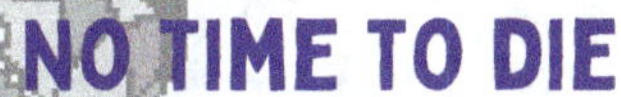

NO TIME TO DIE

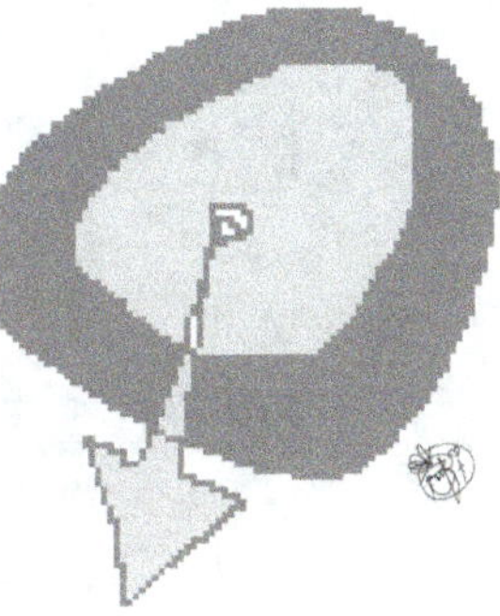

NO TIME
NO TIME
TO
WONDER
WHY
.....

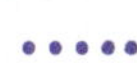

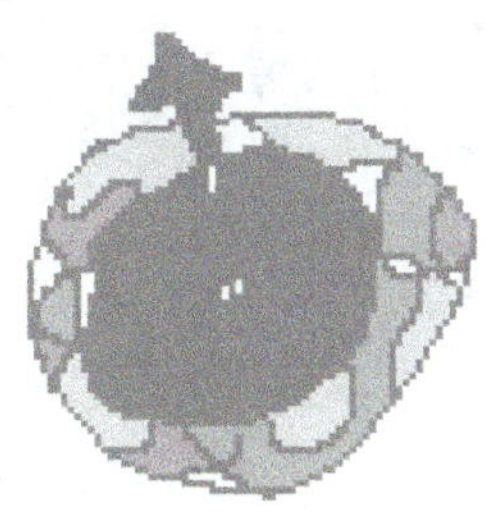

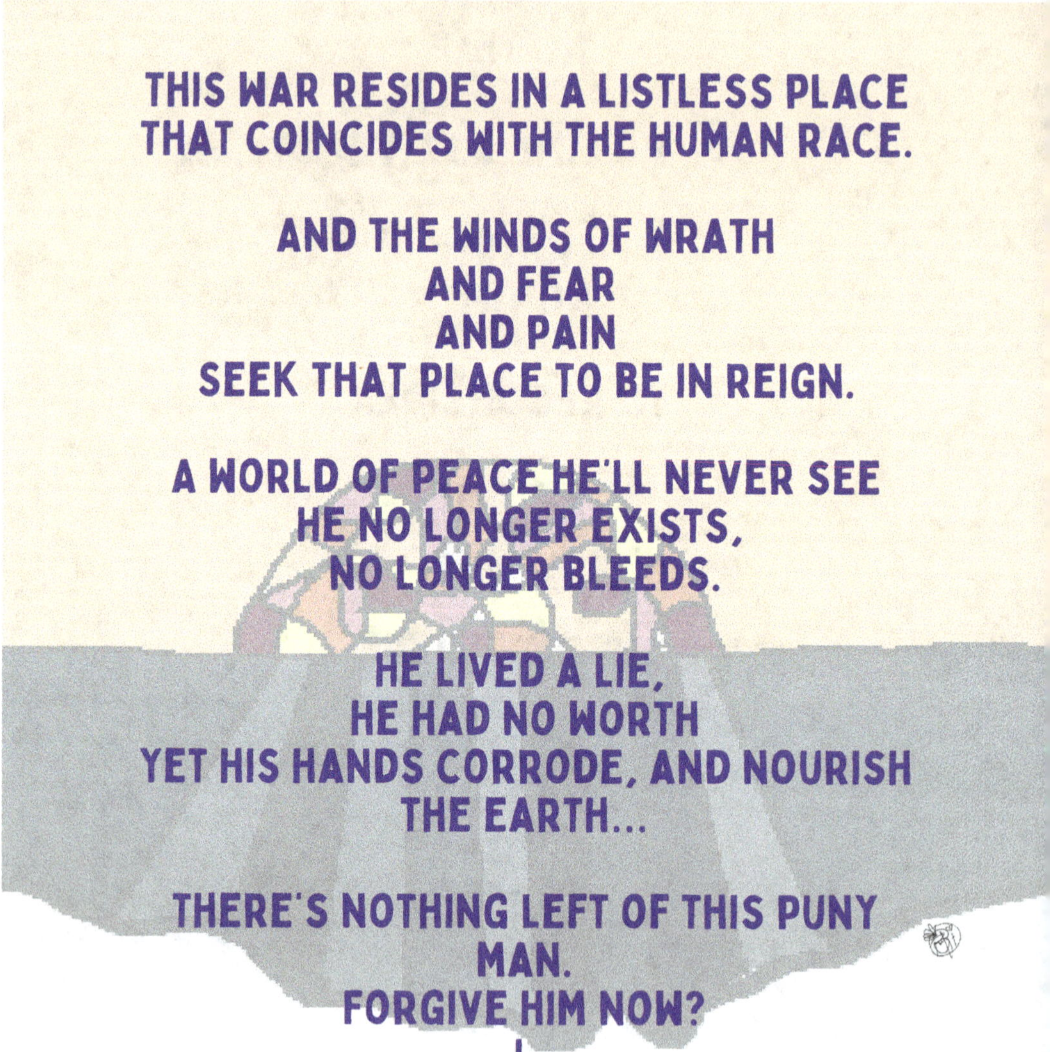

THIS WAR RESIDES IN A LISTLESS PLACE
THAT COINCIDES WITH THE HUMAN RACE.

AND THE WINDS OF WRATH
AND FEAR
AND PAIN
SEEK THAT PLACE TO BE IN REIGN.

A WORLD OF PEACE HE'LL NEVER SEE
HE NO LONGER EXISTS,
NO LONGER BLEEDS.

HE LIVED A LIE,
HE HAD NO WORTH
YET HIS HANDS CORRODE, AND NOURISH
THE EARTH...

THERE'S NOTHING LEFT OF THIS PUNY
MAN.
FORGIVE HIM NOW?
I
THINK
I
CAN.

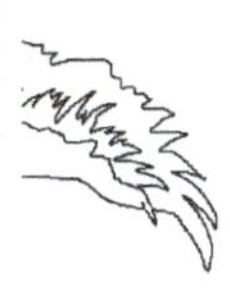
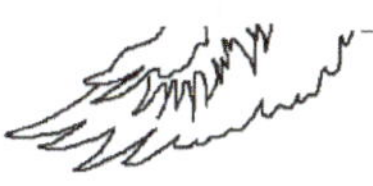
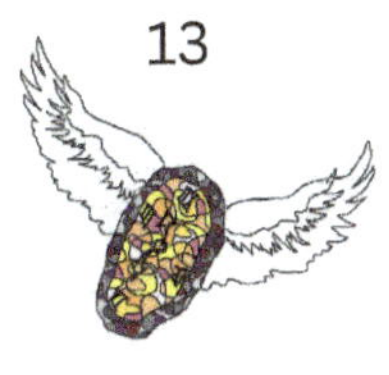

FORGIVE, FORGIVE

FORGIVE HIS LIFE

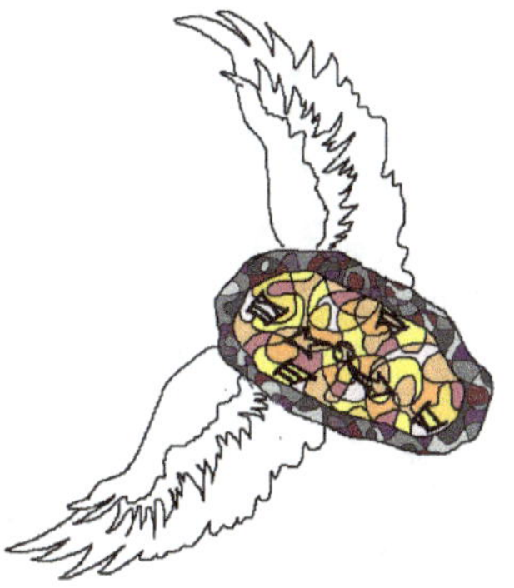

FORGIVE
FORGIVE

HE LIVED IN STRIFE

FORGIVE
FORGIVE

FORGIVE,
AND YOU

WILL FIND

you

need

Forgiveness

too

....

1984, 17 yrs old

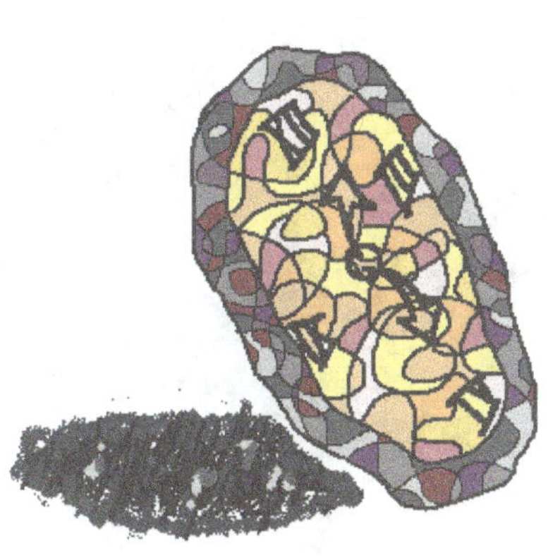

BIGGER.

Rock.
Solid in my soul.
Bearing witness without seeing.
Many lives.
It rests in me
Unthreatening
Unbeckoning
Just rests.
It is a little heavy...
As I carry it with me.

What do I know?
It is bigger than me
This life.

Today
Tomorrow
I live.
Now.
Now is bigger than me
Who am I?
It is not about me
This moment.
I have this moment
In the palms of my hands
This moment
Exists
even without me.

10/11/90
22 yrs old

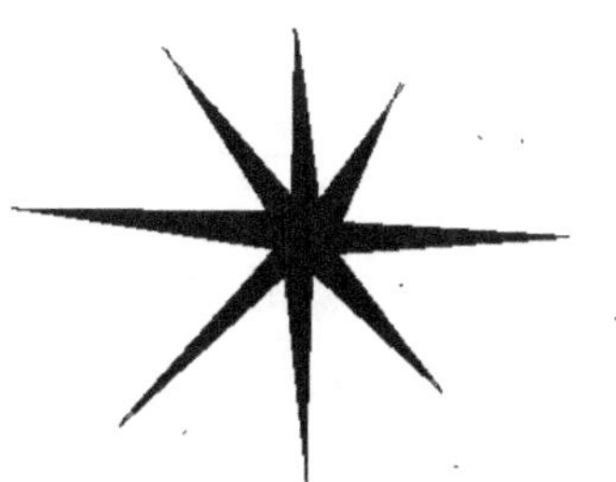

STARSHINE

Starshine!
Blow in my ears!
Starshine,
What do I hear?

Freely
You wait
For what
You need not say
But your breath
Is in me
And frees me
I say

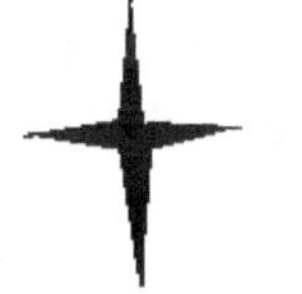

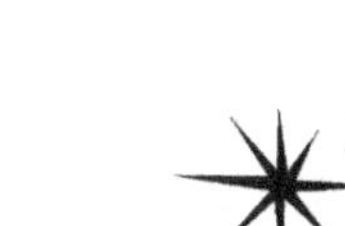

The breath
Is the spoken
A breeze
Of one voice
That comes from
My mouth
That comes from
My choice

A starshine
Is bigger
Than I'll ever be
No boundries
No limits
Room to be free

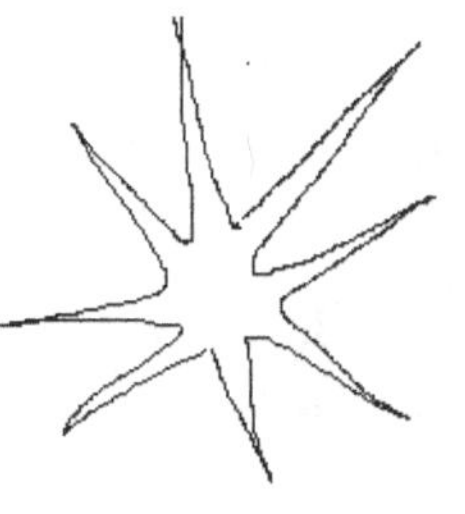

As I listen to starshine
Its voice is my own
I say it
I be it
I let it be known.

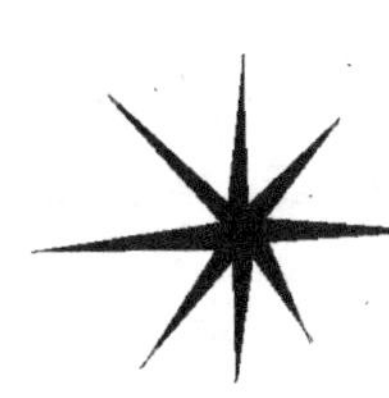

1-26-91
23 yrs old

RUN DOWN

LETTING MY FEELINGS RUN ME DOWN.
NOT HIT AND RUN.
-THEY RUN ME DOWN
THEN THEY FOLLOW ME
EVERYWHERE I GO
AND RUN ME DOWN AGAIN.

AND AS I PEEL MYSELF OFF THE PAVEMENT
I'VE LEFT A LITTLE BIT OF ME
INGRAINED IN THE GRAVEL
AT EACH SITE OF THE CRIME

I'M A PILE OF MOVING PUZZLE
MISSING PIECES.
AND I FEEL SO STRONG WITH WHAT I'VE GOT
UNTIL I'M REMINDED THAT I AM NOT WHOLE
AND SHAMEFULLY I WAIT

FOR THE RUN DOWN.

AND I PICK MYSELF BACK UP.

EVERYTHING SEEMS TO RUN IN CYCLES
LIKE A DOG CHASING ITS TAIL WITH GREAT INTENT.

HOW DO I GO FORWARD?

2-9-91
24 yrs old

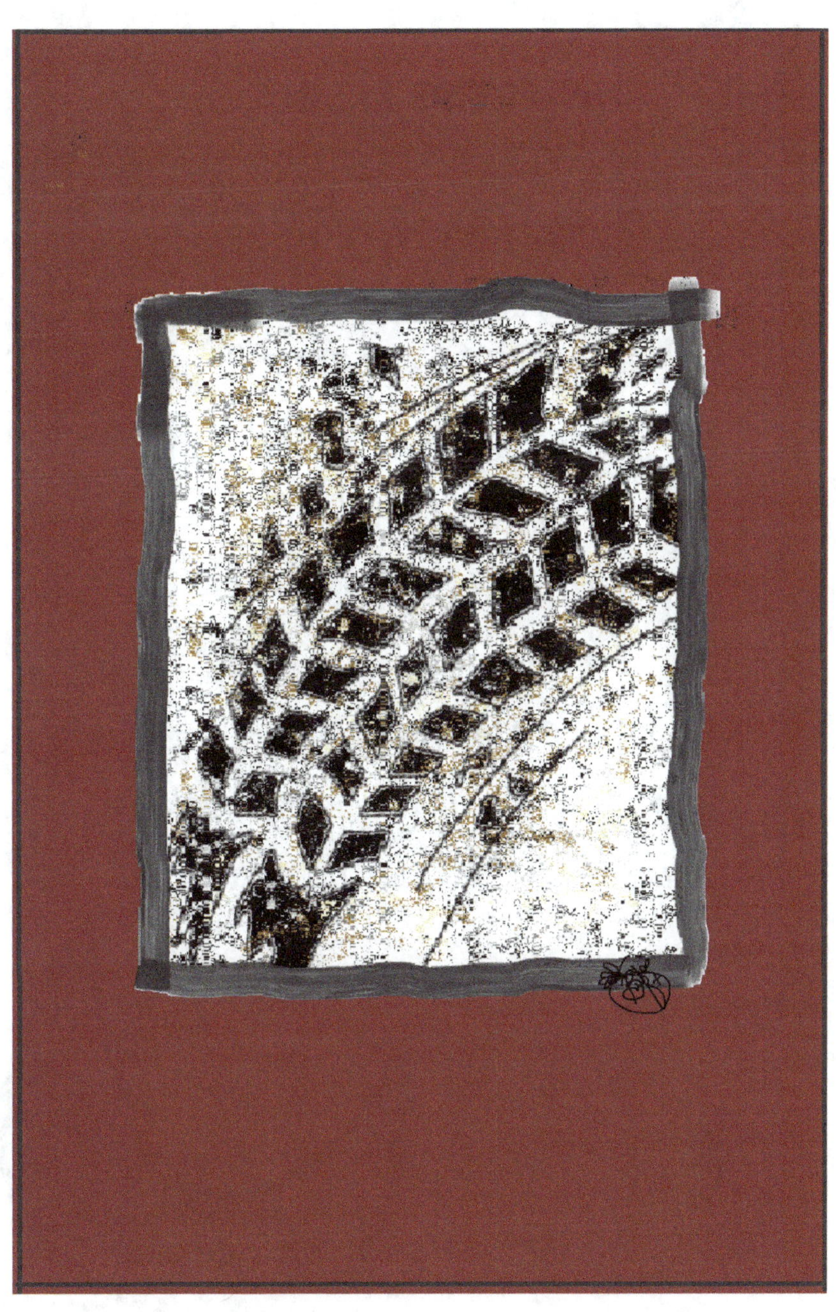

HAPPINESS PHOBIA....

Oh, how I fear, HAPPINESS
That inevitable, so recognizable
LOSS OF CONTROL!
That sends one into FRENZIED FITS
of SMILES!!!!!
And God forbid — LAUGHTER!!!!
Oh how I revel in my skill
To control my smile,
To tactfully entertain with my laughter,
Oh what a blissfully unhappy soul am I

5/3/87
19 yrs old

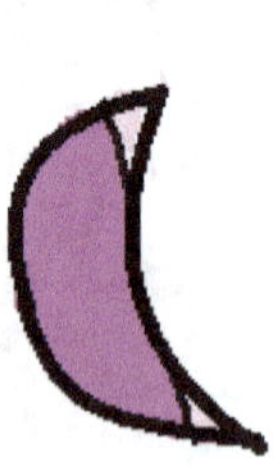

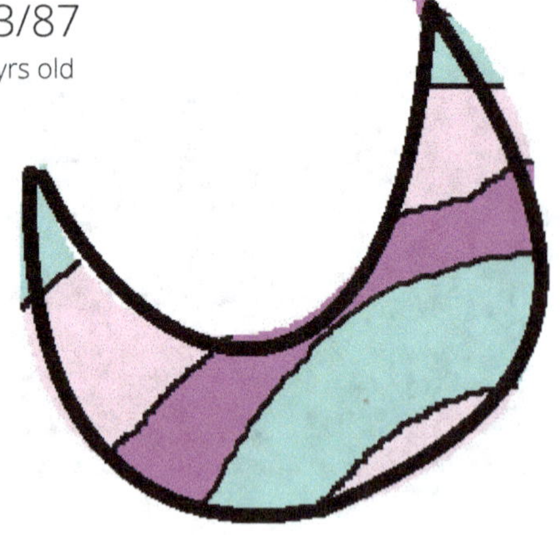

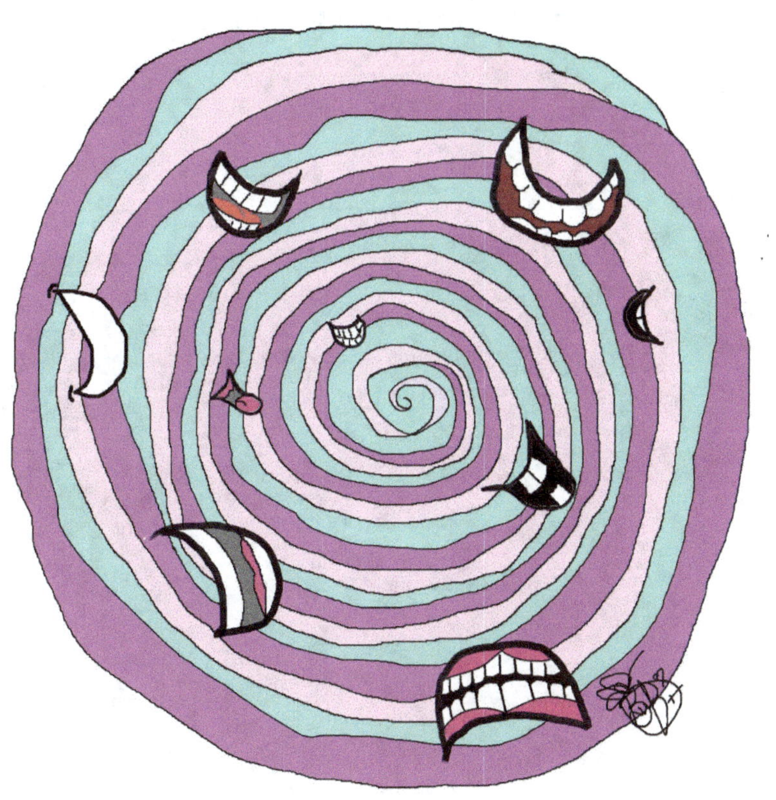

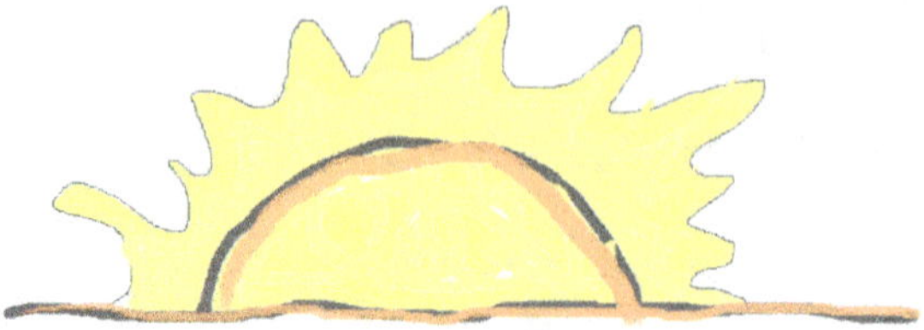

THE WAYWARD FLOWERS

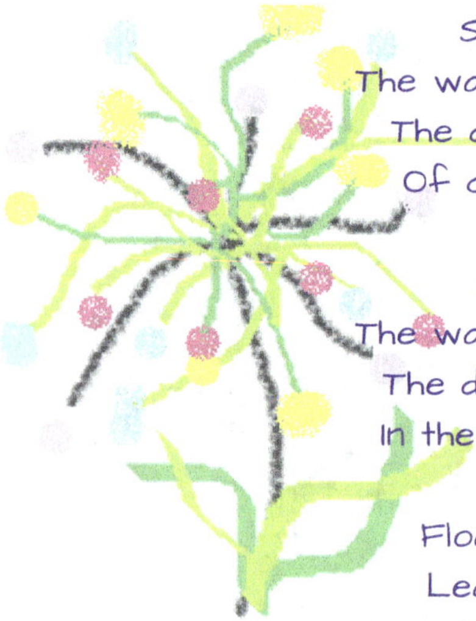

Sit amidst
The wayward flowers
The drifting hours
Of castaway lies

Sit aside
The wayward flowers
The drifting hours
In the limitless skies

Floating in mind
Leaving behind
Footsteps
And thoughtless lies.

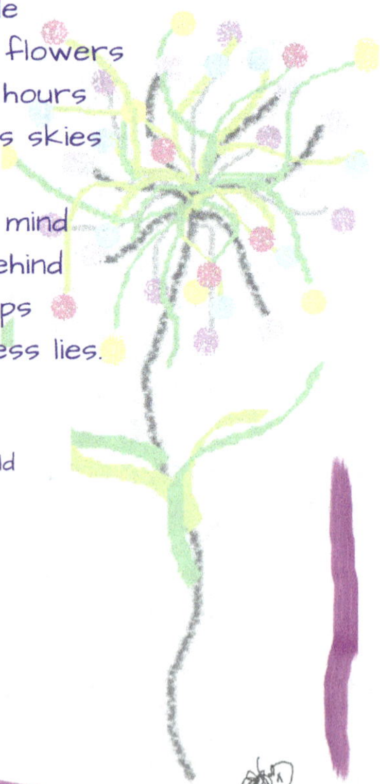

12-1-90
23 yrs old

The peace within
Is
So
Very
Quiet.
And speaks only
When it wants to.
The peace
Within
Is a warm
Nurturing
Tide
In harmony with
An ocean
Of many directions.
My peace within
Is whole
Healthy
And wise.

I am my peace within.

1/26/87
20 yrs old

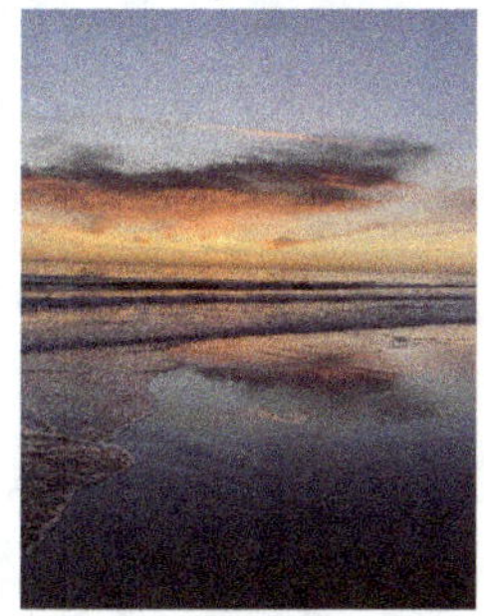

Take my advice.

TOSS IT

A heart in motion
a mind in freeze
manmade commotion
so hard to please
the grand
the bold
the lies
that are told
to our heart
like a talented carnival vendor
making us believe we need things we don't
and should do things we won't
We walked away
with a prize
we didn't need.
How hard it is
to ignore
that big stuffed monkey
on the bed.
How much harder it is to finally toss it.
Toss away that thing we don't need
toss away that thing that brings grief
we thought we should follow its lead
but the joy was brief
and we were left
with grand
bold
lies

filling our space
and diverting our eyes
from the true beauty around us.
Toss it.
keep the heart in motion.
let the mind be in creation
living life is the one solution
where giving is keeping
and it comes to fruition
when all is lost
to subtract is addition.
To toss it,
is to have what matters the most.
Freedom. And love.
~ To all who have struggled and learned to
let go...

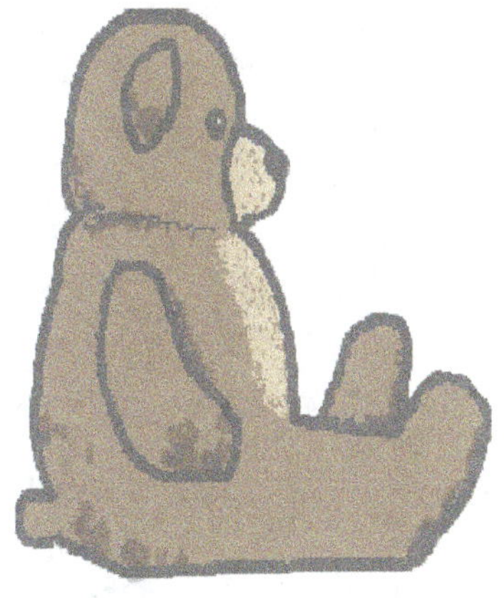

Love, mom.

I love you,
I want you to be the BEST you
can be
every moment of your life
is an investment
your 'rainy day' fund
your 'vacation' fund
your 'in case of emergency'
fund
in your big
beautiful
brain
that God gave you
it has whosawhatzits
and thingamajiggers
that are just WAITING
for you to figure them out
WAITING for discovery
to bring you JOY
and HEALTHY PRIDE
in yourself
and your life!!
To equip you with skills
and gifts
for yourself
in ABUNDANCE
so that you can also
BLESS OTHERS
with your skills
and your gifts
...

I am trying to lead you to
those places
trying to wake you
when you're sleeping
nudge you when you're
laying
guide you when you're
standing still
provide for you
when you're ready to move
be there for you
when you fall
from those mountains you try
to climb
SO WAKE!
STAND!
WALK!
LEARN!
CLIMB!!
I cannot do ANYTHING for
you,
until you do these things for
yourself!!!

I love you
and that
AMAZING
STRONG
GENIUS
CREATIVE
young man
that you are

Am I so selfish
for wanting
myself
you
and the world
to see that man in action??

xo
mom
2021

POSSIBLE TRUTH
There's a certain thing
A thought
An idea
Possibly a truth
I'm thinking
Forming
Possibly learning
In my head.
In my thoughts.
In my heart and soul.
And hopefully in my life.
Maybe even in yours.
Floating in front of me
Around me
Above me
Like dust
Caught in the sunlight.
Like a seed,
buoyant in the stream of my life
Maybe even yours.
It's barely beyond my grasp
As I gently reach for it
And it gracefully dances
Between my fingertips
And floats away again.
....something about freedom.
And love.
And choice.
And empowerment.
Something about commitment
Without attachment;
It requires freedom,
Allows love,
Presents choice,
And leads to empowerment.
I'm not even sure if I'm meant to catch it at all.
Perhaps it's efficacy lies only in its own freedom...
But I'd like to know
This possible truth.
For me.
And maybe even for you.

2016? 49 yrs old

WHEN I DIE

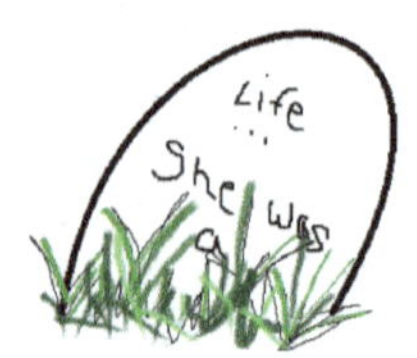

And when I die
And buried I will be
And all my friends
Encircle around me
In a box lowered in to a ditch,
Will my tombstone say,
"Life, she was a bitch!"?

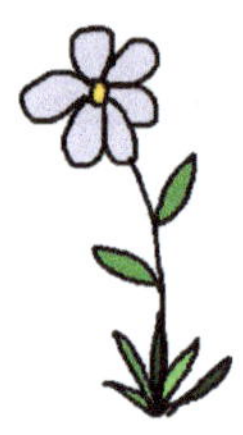

And when I die
While standing with you
My eyes glazed over
My being through
A bigger quote's needed
Lest my tombstone say
"Life? You mean, today?"

My tombstone should read
"No more to say
No game left to play
No words left unspoken
Each action a token
Towards an insight
A light
Always bright."
Life? No time to talk, I'm livin' now!

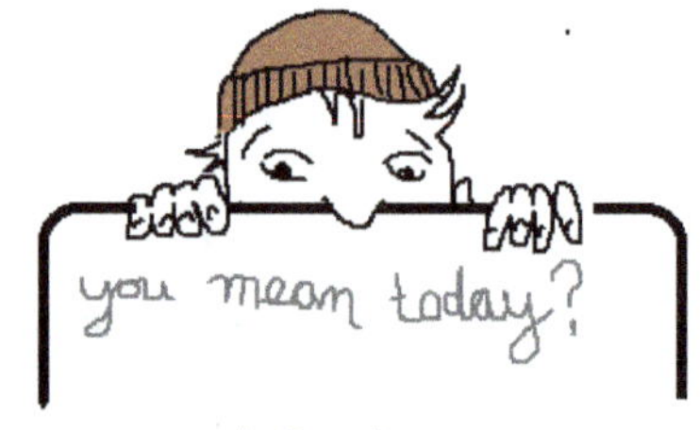

And if I die
With all my rights intact
My right to say 'I can't'
My right to react
I'll take them with me
And my 'potential' too
And the world will keep living
And so will you.

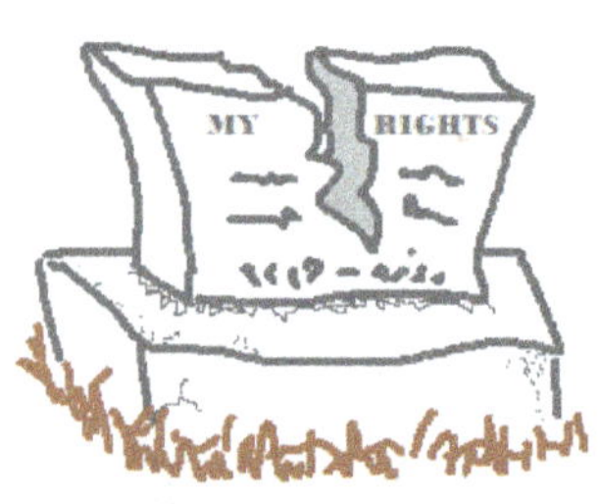

What do I want
my tombstone to say?
How about, 'don't cry...
today
was a good day to die'...

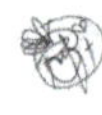

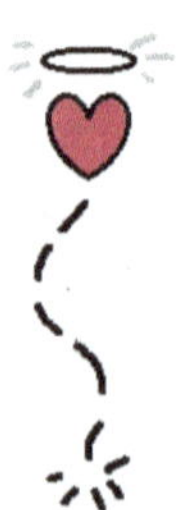

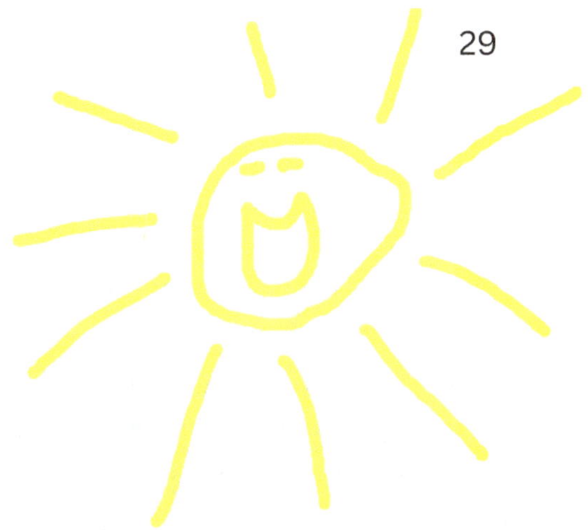
No time to work!
I'm Livin' NOW!

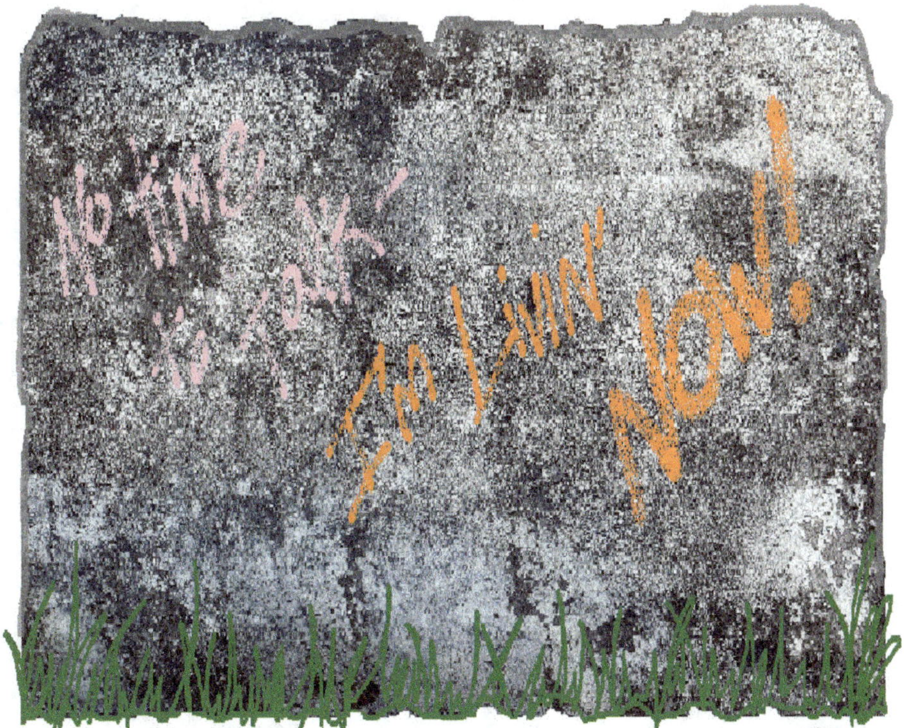

There was a point in my life when I realized I had been living under the illusion that life was suppossed to

be *easy*.

Once I embraced the idea that

life would often be **hard**,

It suddenly became easier.

a paradox.

date uncertain. 2013 perhaps

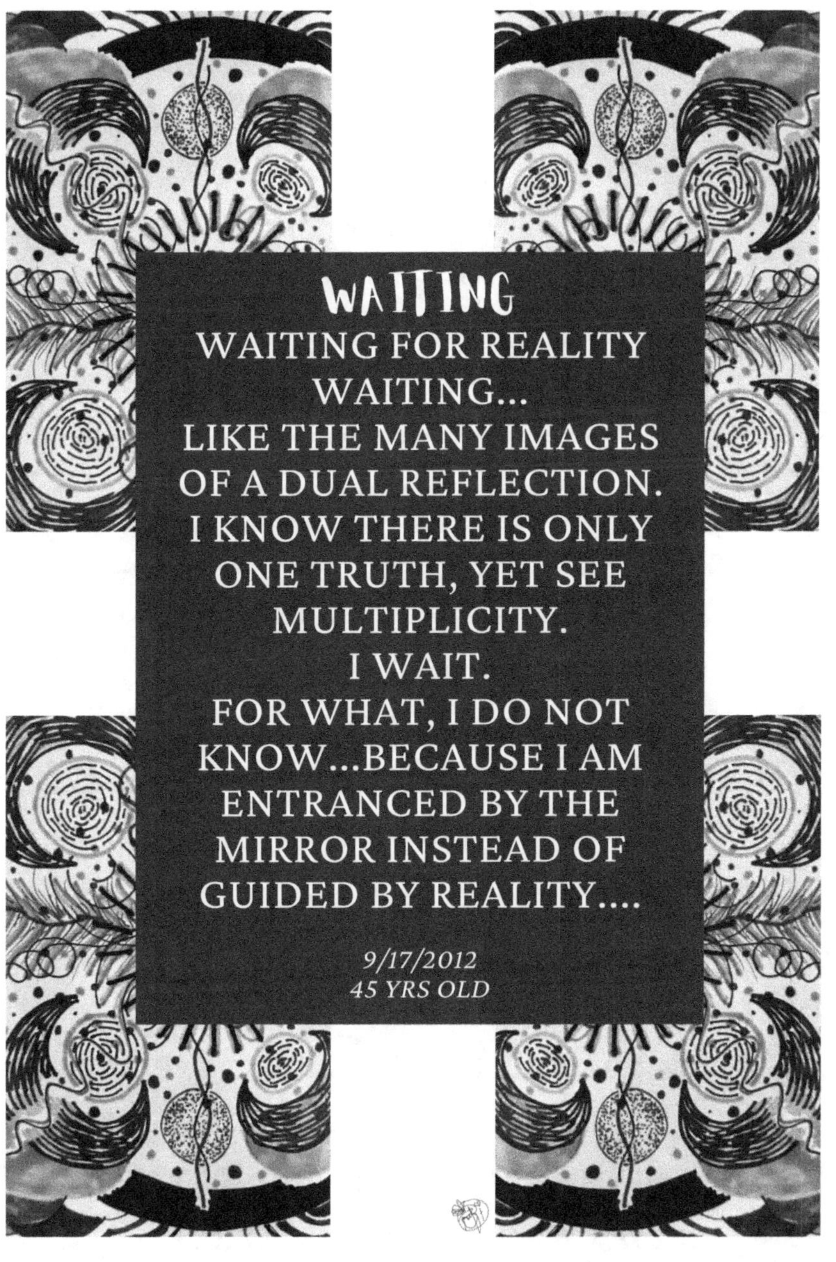

WAITING
WAITING FOR REALITY
WAITING...
LIKE THE MANY IMAGES
OF A DUAL REFLECTION.
I KNOW THERE IS ONLY
ONE TRUTH, YET SEE
MULTIPLICITY.
I WAIT.
FOR WHAT, I DO NOT
KNOW...BECAUSE I AM
ENTRANCED BY THE
MIRROR INSTEAD OF
GUIDED BY REALITY....

9/17/2012
45 YRS OLD

BURN TO LEARN

deep
real
sometimes opaque.
heavy
burden
sometimes heartbreak.
reaching out
with arms at my side
I strained and I yearned
God knows I tried.
tried to try.
tried to trust.
tried to leave the agoraphobic sphere
but it was a bust.
as I sat
and collected dust.
in my all too familiar world.
surrounded by
my all to familiar clutter.
couldn't walk out the door
couldn't open the shutter.

reaching
yearning
to see what was outside
no matter how hard
I just cried.
so I knew,
I had to burn the house down.
to escape it
I had to destroy the walls
of the fortress
turned prison.
I had to leave no option
but to be outside
not in
the box
that had trapped my heart for so many years.
Only then,
could I be free
from the fears
again.

Sorry for the burn, you needed out too.
It wasn't a good place for anybody anymore
..... for me, or you.

11-15-14
46 yrs old. Shortly after divorce.

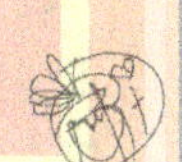

I find myself aimlessly evading sleep again tonight.
I asked myself why,
and this was my answer:

RIGHT WHERE I AM

2/4/21 257 am
Covid isolation.
54 yrs old.

I NEED SOMETHING TO GIVE ME A SENSE OF COMPLETION.

LIKE,

THERE!

I'M DONE!

THERE'S NO MORE TO DO

I'M SET

I'M THROUGH

BUT

I DON'T KNOW WHERE TO STOP

I CAN'T SEEM TO REACH

THE TOP

... IS THERE ONE??

THERE HAS TO BE!

BUT I'M TOO BUSY

TO STOP AND SEE

TOO FOCUSED TO LOOK

TOO WORRIED

TO CARE

ENOUGH

ABOUT FINDING
THE TRAIL
THE MAP
THE SIGNS
THE GENERAL INSTRUCTIONS
THAT MAYBE SAY
THE ELEVATION
ANY INDICATION
THAT I'M GOING
THE RIGHT
DIRECTION.

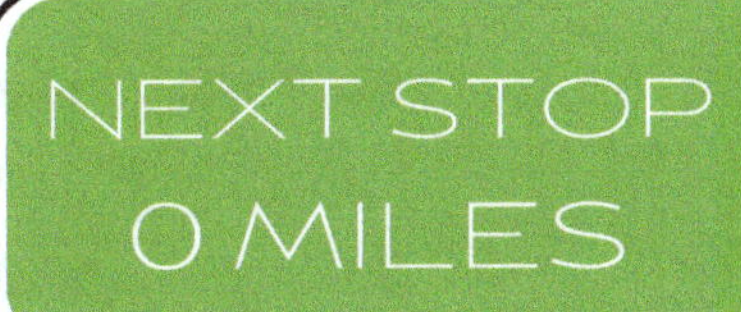

Or where am I even going??

JUST
WHERE DO I STOP?
AM I CLIMBING
TO REACH INSPIRATION POINT?
OR MAYBE
THAT VIEW
THAT PLACE
THE DESTINATION
DIDNT NEED A SIGN
A TRAIL
A MAP
MAYBE IF I STOPPED TO SEE
I'M RIGHT WHERE
I'M MEANT TO BE.
SO STOP.
AND BE
INSPIRED
RIGHT WHERE
I
AM.

WRONG
WAY

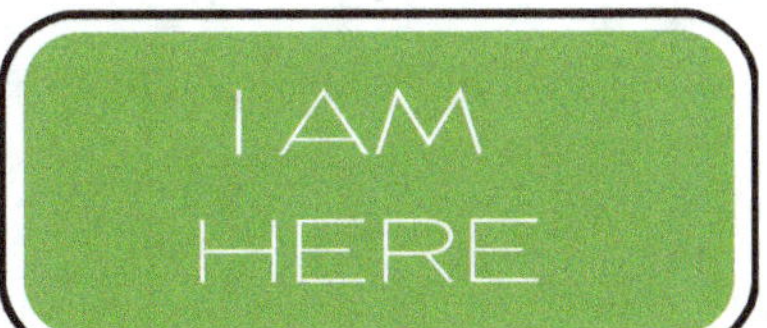

..... GOOD NIGHT 💜 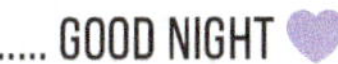

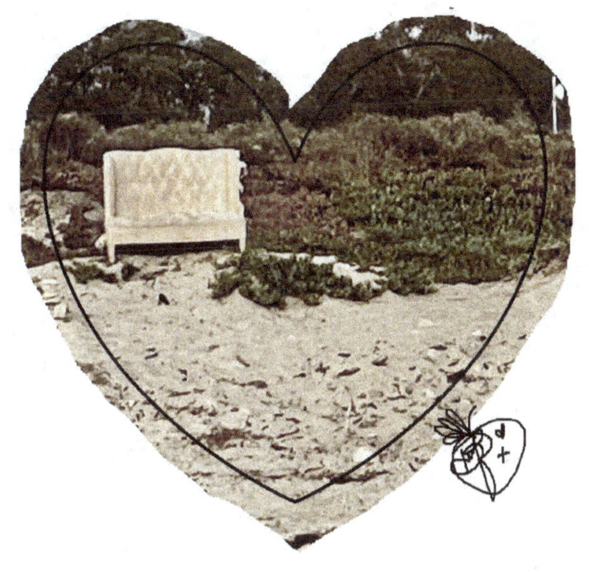

Feelin' Frisky

WHEN TIME COMES
AND FLIES RIGHT BY
AND TRIES TO TAKE FROM YOUR LIPS
MY LONGING FILLED SIGH

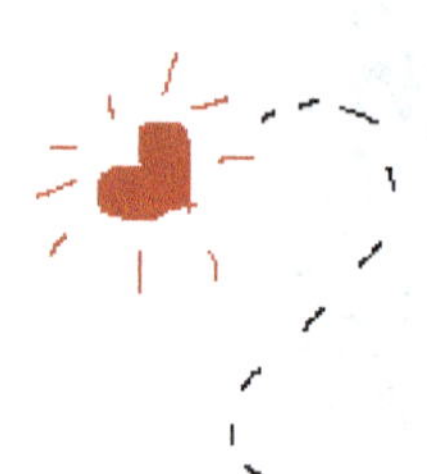

I'LL REACH OUT AND GRAB IT
TAKE IT BACK
IT CAME FROM YOUR LIPS
AND IT'S RIGHT ON TRACK

IT WAS HEADING FOR ME
I'M THE LOVE THAT YOU SEE
THAT SIGH OF LONGING
BELONGS TO ME

LOVE ME
DESIRE ME
WANT ME
ENTIRELY

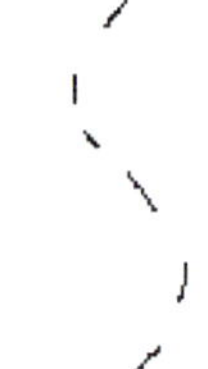

THE SIGH IS FOR ME, AND I'M YOURS

AND WHEN TIME COMES
AND SETTLES THE DAWN
AND IT'S TIME TO PART
AND MY HEART IS ON

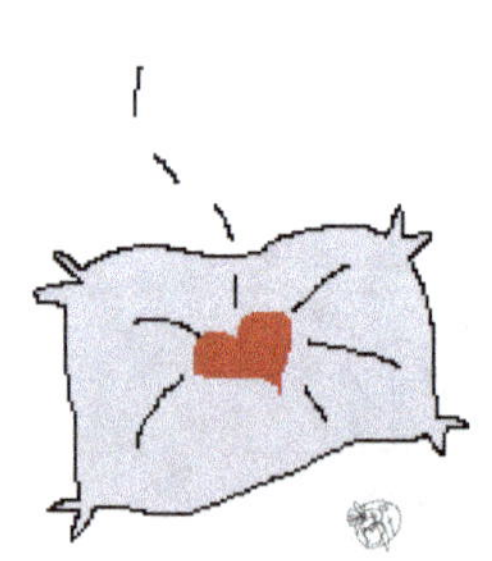

MY SLEEVE

PLEASE TAKE IT
AND HOLD IT
AND MAKE IT YOUR OWN
PUT IT ON YOUR PILLOW
LET IT BE KNOWN

IT'S YOURS, MY HEART IS YOURS

AND THE TIME WILL COME AFTER DAYS OF
UNREST
OF LOVING AND LEAVING; BEING PUT TO
THE TEST
STRAINING TO NOT EXPLODE WHEN WE ARE
APART
LAUGHING WHEN YOU KISS MY LIPS AND
CRYING WHEN YOU TOUCH MY HEART

THE TIME WILL COME
WHEN WE'VE NO MORE GOODBYES
WHEN LIFE BINDS US TOGETHER
WHEN WE COMPLETE OUR TIES

OF LOVE
AND BEAUTY
AND LONGING
AND DESIRE

AND WE'LL GIVE OUR LIVES
NEW MEANING
FULLY KINDLE THE FIRE

THAT BEGAN FOR US
WHEN TIME WAS NEW
AND NOW IT'S TIME FOR ME AND YOU

TO GIVE OURSELVES FREELY
COMPLETELY
AND PURELY

AND LOVE IN A WAY
THAT TOMORROW OR YESTERDAY

WILL NEVER BOTHER US AGAIN
NOW TIME CANNOT STOP US
TODAY WE WIN

4-29-09

42 yrs old

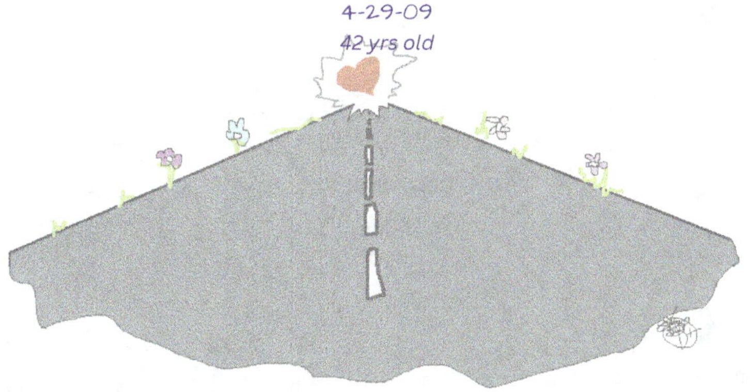

STRONGER.

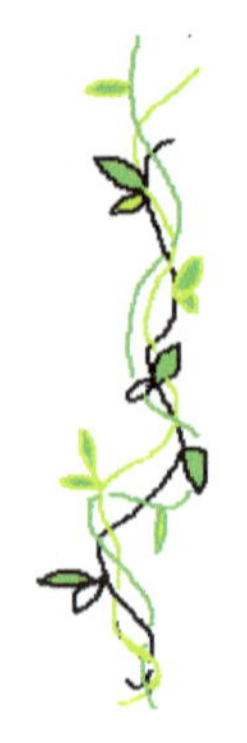

STRONGER
IS THAT THE WAY IT GOES?
I THOUGHT IT WAS MORE LIKE
ENERGY
INERTIA
FADING AS IT FLOWS
BUT THIS??
IT'S NOT LIKE
A BALL ROLLING
THAT EVENTUALLY
WITH FRICTION
WILL STOP
IT'S MORE LIKE
A BATTERY
AND ALTERNATOR
THERE'S NO BOTTOM
NO TOP
NO LIMIT
TO THIS LOVE
YES
I SAID IT
ITS TRUE
THERE'S A PURITY
OF ME
AND YOU
THAT EMITS
IT'S OWN POWER
SPARKED
AND FANNED
INTO FLAME
BY THIS GIFT
FROM GOD

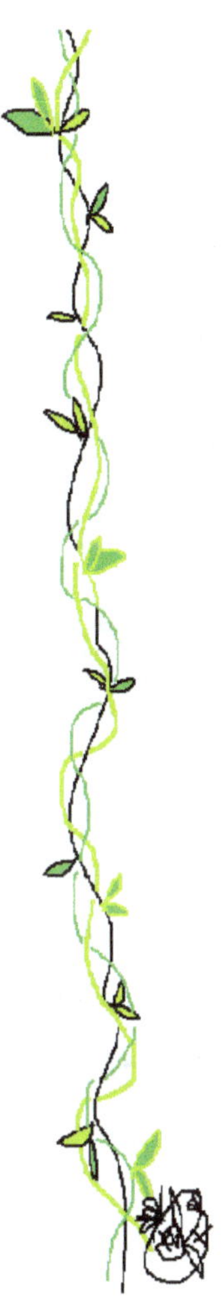

IT'S AS IF

WE ARE THE SAME

SPIRIT

THE SAME HEART

WE ARE ART

IN PROCESS

BEAUTY

NEVER ENDING

GETTING STRONGER

FROM THE START.

WE ARE LOVE.

WE ARE WHOLE

WE ARE FOREVER

A CRUCIAL ROLE

IN A LIFE

BOUND TOGETHER

BY GRACE

AND SERENDIPITY

CONNECTED

BONDED

EMBRACED

IN SURETY

CAN'T STOP

WON'T STOP

THIS BALL IS ROLLING

THIS LOVE IS GROWING

STRONGER

EVERYDAY.

7-15-2020 53 yrs old. new love, eventually married :)

42

OPEN SEASON FOR LOVE!

Feeling love again!

love

For all

For you

For me

I return

To being free

This isn't about just you or

me

Open my heart again

Open my eyes again

Open my hands again

Open my arms again

to love someone

to gaze in someones eyes

to touch,

to hug and hold....

3-27-09

*41 yrs old. Just before
leaving my ex-husband.*

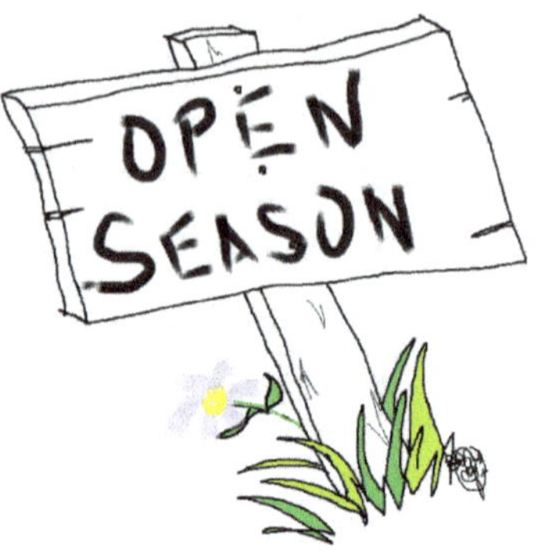

Open it all for you and me

No more closed doors

No more locks

let your knocks ring in my memory

...just come in!

Come warm my heart

Come in!

Come take my hand

Come in!

laugh with me

love with me

Cry with me

And when we can see with our eyes closed

When we can touch

Though far apart

When we can find peace in the noise

And sing in the silence

Then we have loved...

MY THING

you're the split to my peas
the butter to my fly
the sun to my flower
the Apple to my pie

the avo to my cado
the Su to my shi
the beauty to my full
the hap to my py

you're my something
my one thing
my that thing
my this thing
my great things
my new things
my sweet thing
my hot thing

you are my tomorrow
You are my today
you'll be my forever
you'll be my yesterday

my hopes
my wins
my first place
second place
third place
my entire race

my run
my rest
my sleep
my dance
my for sure
my best chance
my let's try
my let's pass that by
my health
my resourcefulness
my wealth

you are my love
you are my joy
you are the songs I sing
you
are my every thing!

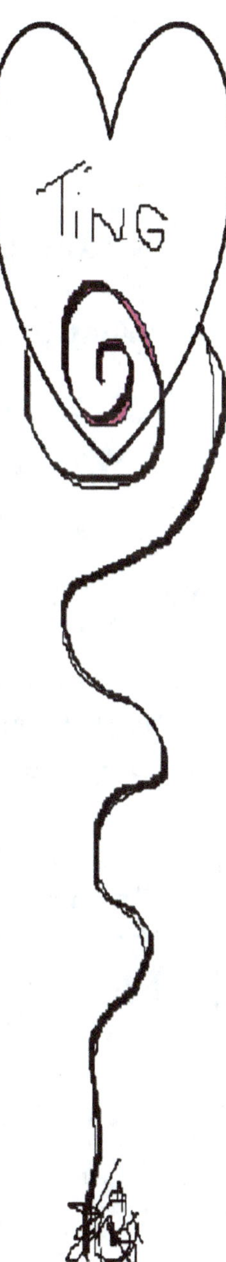

3/31/2021 54 yrs old...thats the guy that I married :)

Our kiss

Here's the question I ask, over and over
again:
Whats the point? Do we ever win?

It's in all of life, but what I ask is this:
Why is there so much power,
In a kiss?

I can be friends with you, with 10, three or
two
But once our lips meet and this we repeat
The rules are changed it's a new game
Filled with sorrow, joy, pride and shame...

We run together full of glee
Then walk and bask in loves glory
Then wonder why the road's so long
And hold our sides, bending over, saying
we can't go on...

...until the next kiss, the next lips,
the next road...
And we run again, with a different load...

Can it ever be truly different?
Is it just a bunch of roads with destinations
And when we reach the end
We find new temptations?

Is it possible to never stop walking?
Or when we reach a dead end
U turn and keep talking?

Is there math to this?
Is there reason?
Is love allowed to last?
Can it?
Or does it just clump into seasons?

And can these seasons be lived
By the same two
That once upon a time kissed
And became me and you?

2-4-10
43, pondering my
lonely marriage.

The Island of Us

Now here we are
At that place
You know the one?
No?
Oh, I get it,
It's because we've never been here before!
Isn't it gorgeous??
And the views are AMAZZZZINGGG!!!
The air pressure is different here too...
Have to frequently take in a deep breath
To fill my lungs
Cuz it takes my breath away.
And it squeezes my heart.
I get up here,
With you,
And I am surrounded by the blue
Of you
Your eyes
And the breeze
Of you
Your sweet breath
As you sweetly kiss me
And my heart
Releases
When you hold me
Ever so gently

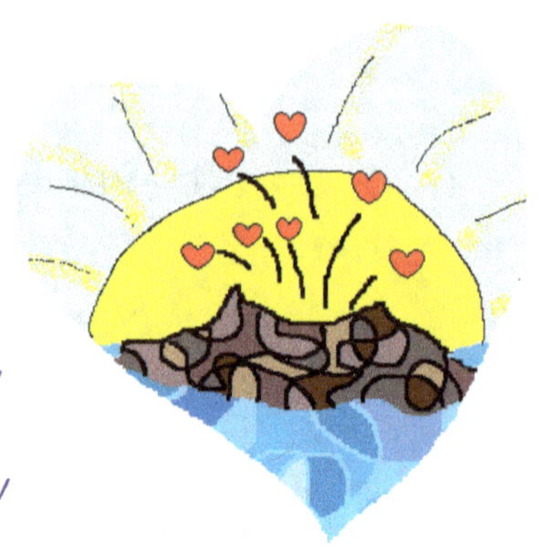

....and I feel the warmth
wanting to boil
And I feel the strength
Wanting to roil
like the earth
moving beneath our entwined bodies.
I think we found a volcano
And it's created
The island of us.
I can hardly wait
To watch it grow
And change
Teeming with life
Creating it's own weather.
The soft rains
And the tumultuous hurricanes
The bold sun
And the cold
We will brave
In each others arms
As we watch our island
Become a paradise.

6-16-20
53 yrs old
falling in love again.

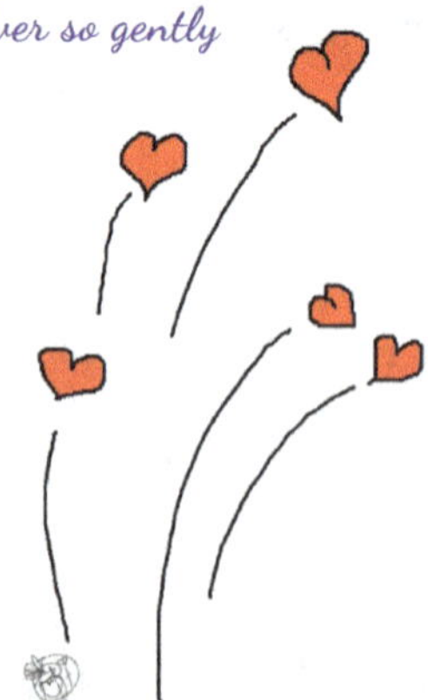

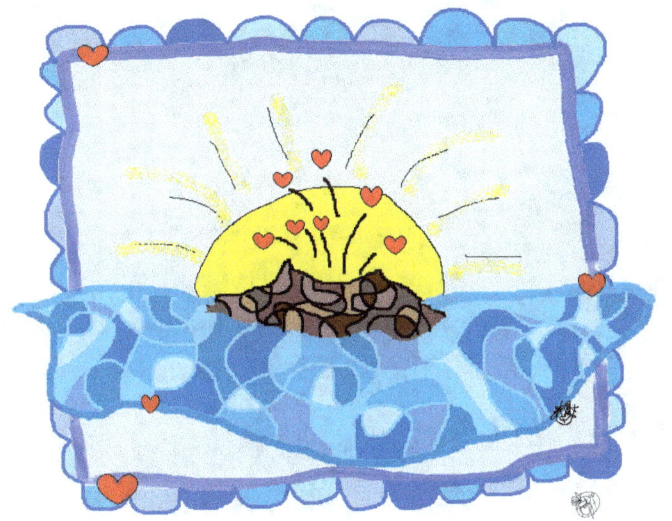

UNSTABLE STAR

SUNSHINE.
BRIGHT.
WARM
NURTURING...
...HOT.
BLINDING,
SCORCHING....
WHO AM I?
WATCH OUT
IF I AM NEAR.
I POSSESS
THE POWER TO HEAL
THE POWER TO FEEL
THE POWER TO INSPIRE
THE POWER TO LIFT HIGHER
THE POWER TO BURN
WHEN IS IT MY TURN
TO HAVE THE POWER TO LOVE
WITHOUT CONSEQUENCES...?
TO LOVE WITHOUT THE HEAT
OF THE FEAR TO RETREAT
AN INFINITE UNIVERSE
AND YET
I AM STUCK IN THIS SPOT
GOING NO WHERE
WITH ALL MY GRAVITATIONAL PULL
STILL YOU ARE NOT WITHIN MY REACH
AND EVEN IF YOU WERE
YOU WOULD TURN TO ASH
IN MY HANDS
HOW CAN I HOLD YOU?

LOVING YOU FROM AFAR
LEAVES MY HEART AJAR
I AM NOT THE SUN
I AM NOT THE CENTER OF YOUR UNIVERSE
LOOK UPON ME, PLEASE,
AS IF LOOKING UPON SOMETHING OF BEAUTY
FOR I BURN FOR YOU
BRIGHT, I LIGHT UP WHEN YOU ARE AROUND
WARM, YOU LIGHT A FIRE IN MY SOUL
NURTURING, I LONG TO HOLD YOU AND CARESS
YOU
I AM NOT THE SUN,
PERHAPS I AM MORE OF AN
UNSTABLE STAR.
WILL YOU REMEMBER ME
AFTER I FINALLY EXPLODE
INTO A MILLION BRIGHT PIECES?
SHARDS THAT FLOAT INTO THE UNIVERSE
MAYBE THEN I WILL FEEL THE FREEDOM I LONG FOR
AND MAYBE YOU CAN TAKE A PART OF ME
WITH YOU
AND MAYBE THEN
I CAN BELONG TO YOU
WHEN I SEIZE TO FULLY BELONG AT ALL...

4-6-09
42 yrs old.
Hoping I can save my marriage.

i have questions.....

because why

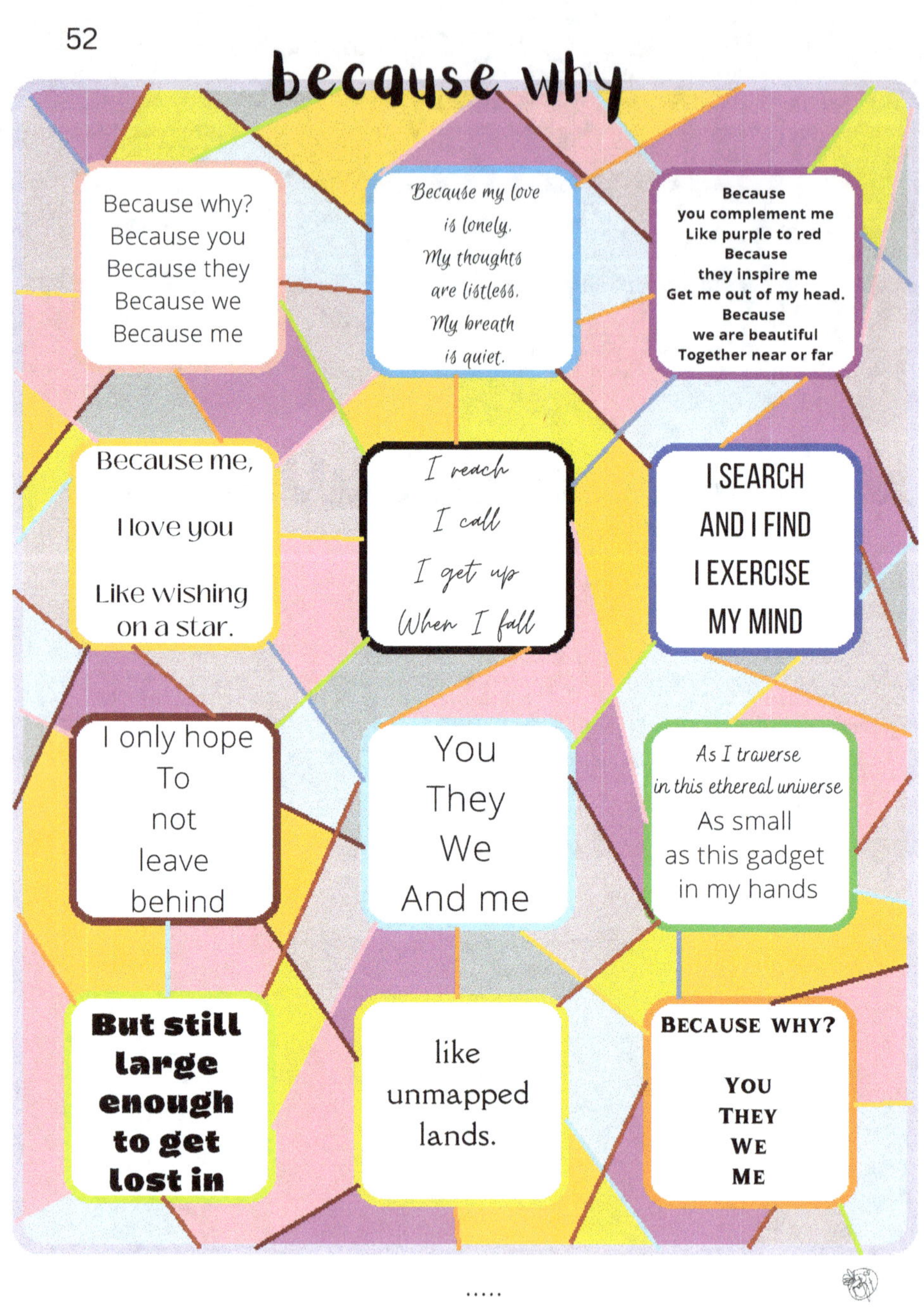

.....
Thats why.

12/29/14
...as a single parent of four children knowing it IS possible to make a good life happen.

WHAT DOES IT MEAN TO BE FREE??

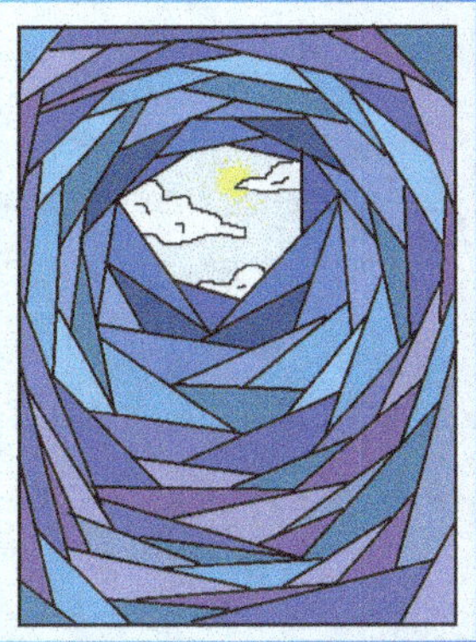

What does it mean to be free?
No obligations?
Buckets of money?
Why does my heart feel so bound?
I thought I understood,
but no theory is sound...
Even love, at its best,
puts us through a test.
And hope ties us to
things often untrue.
What is it to be free?
Perhaps I`ll know
when I see through you,
and begin to see me.

1/5/2012
45 yrs old

 breathing in, breathing out...

Why is it that the more I desire to be beautiful...
the more I want to eat?
rippling streams
And waving grass
Fields of flowers covered in dew.
Sunlight streaming
On glowing clouds
Waves crashing on the beach, and you.
Music flowing
Voices sing
Harmony unifies everything
I'm looking for peace
In the beauty around me
Why can't I find
The beauty inside me?

Breathing in
Breathing out
Hoping to exhale beauty 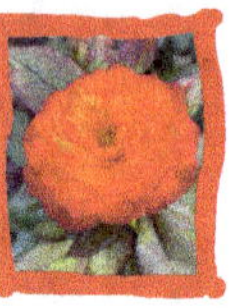 trying to inhale certainty

Breathing out
Breathing in

A rose with its colors
A rose with its form
A rose in its' delicateness
Leaves me forlorn
Longing that I
Could have such allure
A scent to entrance
A beauty so pure

But if God made the flowers
And the caressing breeze
If he made the ocean
Then tell me please
Didn't he make me?

And if God made flame
And waterfalls
If He gave you your gifts
Surely He calls
Me to something?

Breathing in
Breathing out
Hope for tomorrow

Breathing out
Breathing in
Hope instead of sorrow

Breathing in
Breathing out
Filling my lungs
Opening my eyes
To my song that needs to be sung.

To a voice that was given to me
A life given so that I could be free
To break the shackles of pride and shame
And the chains of agonizing self blame

Shame
a siren
A temptation
A lie

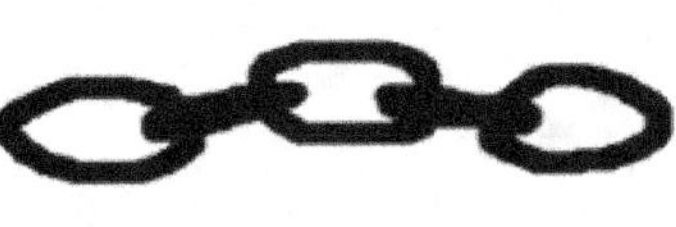

A revelation
Of desire
That leaves me
Imprisoned
Not free

Torn. Between faith and uncertainty
Looking for beauty...
Longing for fealty...
Hurting for surety,
Questioning fidelity.
I am my worst enemy...

Breathing in
Breathing out
Waiting

Breathing out
Breathing in
Hating

This emptiness
Fill me with your breath.
Help me to avoid
The death
That seeks my soul.

4-29-09
42 yrs old. Feeling lost.

Longing, desire, delight.

Why is there comfort in beauty?
How can it be true comfort,
When Satan was Gods most beautiful angel.
So why, when we look upon beauty,
Do we long for more?
Desire to give all?
Delight in it's presence?
Like the sirens of myth,
Who in their beauty
Compel
Then betray
Is there another side to beauty,
Evil hidden
In lust
In wanton passion
In coveting.
In flattery, greed and foolishness.
Is there any good left
In beauty?
Or has Satan claimed it as his own?
Can we take back beauty
Restore it
Like returning to the Garden of Eden?
Or have we lost beauty forever
To the wiles of the devil
And the lusts
Of the flesh...
Longing....
Desire....
Delight....
They fill me
Fill the crevasses
Permeate my soul
Where their absence
Leaves
Aching
Wanting
Irony....
We want to long for something, to feel alive
To desire something, to chase away apathy
And to delight in something, to ignore our eternal sadness.
Maybe that
Is why
Beauty brings us comfort.
Because it creates in us
Longing,
Desire,
And delight.....

2-28-09
42 yrs old. Just trying to understand...!

My brain is full.

FRIEND OR FOE

Odd little machine
Devilish contraption
You lure me in with your promises of
success
Your tease of desires met
My lifeline to a social life,
to connections outside myself,
to knowledge and wisdom,
My lifeline. Period.
Life as I knew it without you is a blur
A series of 'how did I ever' ponderings.
But now my contemplation is on
'how will I ever. ...'
How will I ever truly live,
When I am glued to you,
my little hand held gadget
powered by electricity and a fear of
lonliness.
I call you mine, but really, it is you who
own me....

2014
47 yrs old.

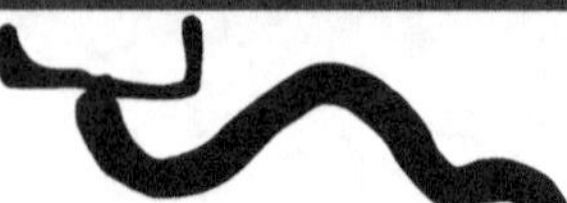

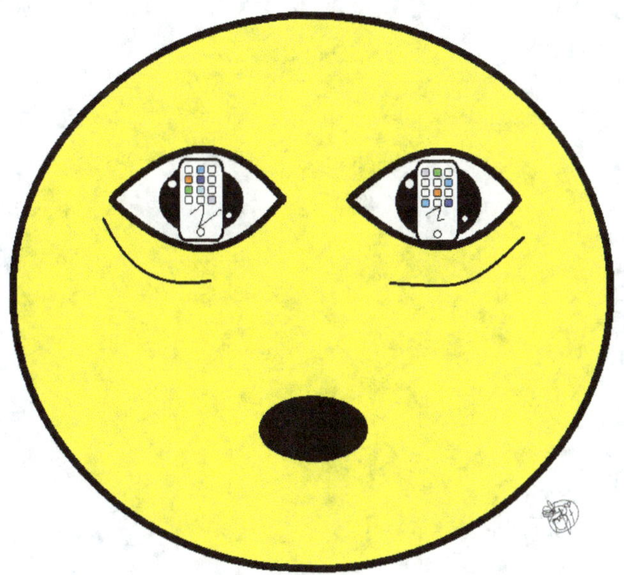

Gone

60 Gone is the woe
that tows
The bliss and freedom
From my breath
Gone is the goodbye to
the sigh
Gone is the fear of death
Here is now
Now and deep
Shallow in thought
As I weep to feel pain.
To try again.
To enjoy the failure
Because I know I can,
I know I can fail.
Gone is the need,
 When the fear is
relinquished.
Gone is the hate, when
obsession leaves
Gone is the love
When fear takes over.
Only to cower
Only to breed
More contempt
No flower to seed
Growth is the pain
That leaves no scars
What is healing?
What is love?
I see no results
If there is no blood.
Give me wounds,
Give me power
To control
and see
And touch
Not this groping in the
dark shit....

I know.

I know nothing lasts forever in this world,
...We all have to die.
I know I there will be times I will hate
Times I will love
Times I will cry.
And I know there are millions of people in this
world
All of us different it's true.
Some I will touch
some will touch me
But none will ever again be you.
So I thank you for your preciousness
And for sharing who you are
And I thank God for sharing you with me
Now that you travel through the stars.
And I hope that there's a heaven
Where we once again can meet
And I know the little time I've known you
has been wonderful and sweet.

2011?
Dedicated to Fred Starner a self titled 'Hobo'
who delightfully made me question my lifes
choices...

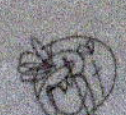

OVERLAPPED.

How many times   I'm writing rhymes
Will I regress   I must confess
Into the void   for all the times
Where time is   I've been depressed
pressed

Will there ever be
A lasting thought
Of anything
I have sought

I search for   there's nothing hiding
nothing

I listen for only
the music of   with silence guiding
silence   ......

I speak to no one   and I am not alone

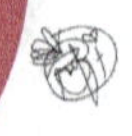

Date uncertain.
early college years.

heartfullness

heartfullness
I am seething heartfullness
My loving has been squeezed
So that now
it has no
Direction but
out
in
All directions

3/2009
42 yrs old
1 year before leaving a
17 year marriage.

Not My Voice

not my voice
not my words
The words I speak are not from me.
The words are formed from words I've heard.

a lifetime of voices.
Like pieces of clay
I've collected them in my soul.
Each piece of clay a different thought
in piece or whole

from different choices
spoken and made
I pick them up as I go
through life, and mold
them together.

Occasionally I spin
something that's worthy of giving
away,
and I start again.
With new clay, and old clay,
new voices and words.

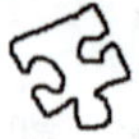
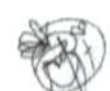

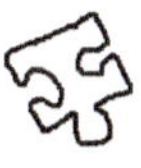

And at times it occurs
like puzzle pieces

And I create a picture I never knew possible
until I got
that last thought
and it all pulls together
as I dutifully wrought
with my hands and mind.

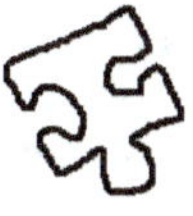

when I speak eloquent,
it is not only my voice.
But 1000 voices.
that came and went and more.
And if you like what you hear,
consider it a choir.
A Choir of 1000 voices.
letting the truth soar

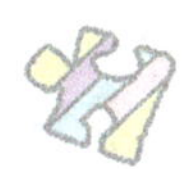
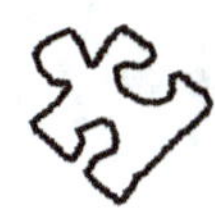

Listen closely,
for you'll likely hear
your voice as well.....

Thank you for that.

3/20/2021
During Covid isolation.

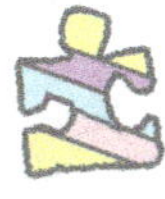

Love Calls Me Home

May 2 2010
43 yrs old
a month before changing the trajectory of my life ...

"Before me lies an ocean, as I stand upon the shore. I have been told I can swim; tread water with my hands and no more...no liferaft, no boat; nothing else to help me float...Just me, and my buoyancy.... And the strength God gave to make me free....So I take a deep breath, and step into the foam, as the water caresses my feet, and Love calls me home...."

A little about the author:

That would be me.

What's there to tell? I was an awkward yet creative and energetic child. And now I'm an awkward yet creative and energetic adult! I had a fair share of struggles in every stage of life. The following are just a few of the groupings of words that got me through it all.

I dislike politics, prefer faith over religeon. I like nature, creating stuff, karaoke, and animals.

Here's me with no makeup and two pair of glasses on my head doing a face-off with my dear sis-out-laws cat. Cuz I have to bug everybodys pets.

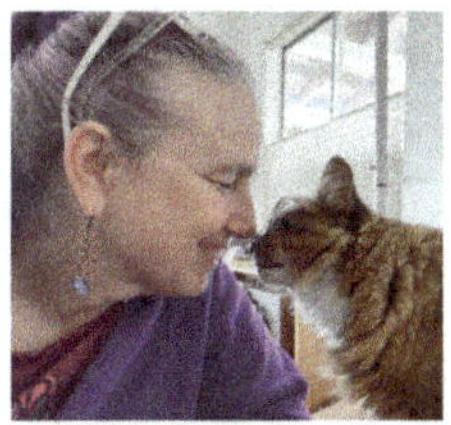

And here's me looking a little more put together; (because that's whats expected).

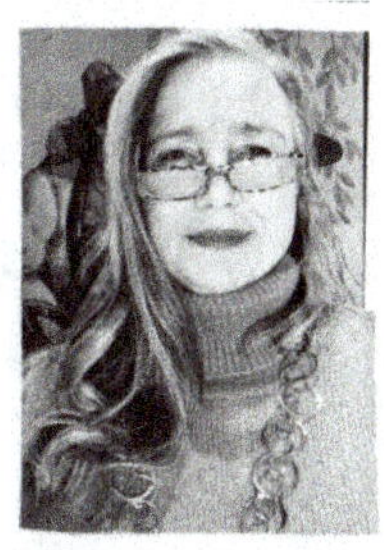

From my "real' to your 'real'...I hope you find a little of yourself in these and future pages.

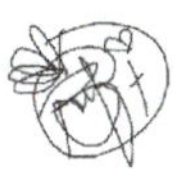